1

- **What different aspects of train travel do they show?**
- **How might the people be feeling?**

- Why might these people be talking to each other?
- How might they be feeling?

Speaking Test Preparation Pack for
Certificate in Advanced English

Acknowledgements

Cambridge ESOL is grateful to the following for permission to reproduce photographs:

Part 2

Travelling by train: Corbis for dining car, Getty Images for crowded train and train in snow.

Face to face: Corbis for old men talking, Getty Images for the therapist, and baseball player arguing with referee.

Part 3

Corbis for market floor of merchant bank, grandfather and grandson playing video game, businesswoman using laptop.

Getty Images for warehouse worker, man working from home and girls using laptops.

Every effort has been made to identify the copyright owners for material used, but it is not always possible to identify the source or contact the copyright holders. In such cases, Cambridge ESOL would welcome information from the copyright owners.

University of Cambridge ESOL Examinations
1 Hills Road
Cambridge
CB1 2EU
UK

www.CambridgeESOL.org

First published 2008
Printed in the United Kingdom by Cambridge Printing Services Ltd
ISBN 978-1-906438-39-5

Contents

Teacher's Notes

Student Worksheets

Introductory Worksheet

Worksheet 1

Worksheet 2

Worksheet 3

Worksheet 4

Supplementary Worksheet

Introduction

This *Speaking Test Preparation Pack for CAE* has been specially created to help you prepare your students for the Speaking test of the Certificate in Advanced English (CAE) from Cambridge ESOL. Written by experienced Speaking test examiners, it consists of:

- a book containing comprehensive Teacher's Notes and a set of six Student Worksheets which provide detailed practice for all parts of the CAE Speaking test
- one set of candidate visuals in colour to allow you and your students to practise with realistic visual stimulus
- a DVD showing real students taking a Speaking test to give your students a clear idea of what to expect on the day.

The Student Worksheets can be photocopied to use in class, or printed from the files on the DVD if you prefer. Worksheets 1–4 cover the four parts of the Speaking test in detail and contain a variety of exercises and discussion tasks using the video on the DVD. The Introductory Worksheet is designed to give students an overview of the whole Speaking test and the Supplementary Worksheet covers how the Speaking test is assessed.

The Teacher's Notes for each worksheet explain in detail how to conduct each activity and provide answers to and commentary on the various exercises. There are also 'Teaching Tips' for each of the four main worksheets, giving you extra ideas for use in class, and 'Helpful Hints for Students' with useful advice for you to pass on.

The DVD contains video of one complete CAE Speaking test for you to use with the worksheets and electronic versions of the Student Worksheets and candidate visuals.

We hope you enjoy using the *Speaking Test Preparation Pack for CAE* and wish your students every success when they take the test.

Cambridge ESOL

CAE Speaking test
Teacher's Notes

■ Aims of the DVD and worksheets

- to raise students' awareness of the format of the CAE Speaking test
- to focus students' attention on techniques that will improve their performance
- to provide opportunities for students to practise the language used in the different parts of the test
- to update teachers on the current test format for the CAE Speaking test
- to provide activities and teaching tips for teachers to use with examination classes.

Please note:

The DVD and worksheets are not intended as a forum for discussing grades. Although in certain questions we are asking students to look at the candidates' performance, it is with a view to improving the students' own performance and not for them to grade the candidates on the DVD.

The CAE Speaking test on the DVD has been produced for teaching purposes only and is not a live exam. There are, therefore, no grades available.

■ How to use the DVD and worksheets

The Student Worksheets are at the back of this book in the section beginning on page 23. The tasks in the worksheets are to be used at your discretion to create maximum benefit for your students. The guidelines below are suggestions only.

You can use the worksheets to:
- introduce the CAE Speaking test at the beginning of your course
- review or revise key points near the exam date
- focus on different parts of the test at different times according to your syllabus.

Please note:

The material is not designed to be used as complete lessons of any fixed length. Make sure that your students are aware when the answers to the tasks cannot be found on the DVD.

Some of your students may find these activities challenging. If necessary, adapt or simplify the tasks and give assistance where needed.

Student's Introductory Worksheet

■ Task One: general information about the CAE Speaking test

Ask the students to fill in the missing information on the worksheet. Tell them they can find some of the information they need on the Candidate Support site at
www.candidates.CambridgeESOL.org/cs/Help_with_exams/General_English/CAE
and in the *Information for Candidates* booklet which they can download.

Answers

1. Length: _____**15**_____ minutes
2. Normal format: _____**2**_____ candidates and _____**2**_____ examiners
3. Number of parts: _____**4**_____
4. The Speaking test is worth _____**20**_____% of the whole CAE exam (all papers).

■ Task Two: what happens in the CAE Speaking test

Ask the students to complete the table on the worksheet with the correct information from the box below.

• leads a discussion • exchanges views and opinions • asks individual direct questions	• expresses opinions through comparing • gives personal information • initiates discussion

Answers

Parts	Timing	What the interlocutor does	What a candidate does	Possible range of language used
1. Interview	3 minutes	**asks individual direct questions**	**gives personal information**	General interactional and social language: • giving personal information about everyday circumstances • expressing opinions • talking about interests and experiences
2. Individual long turn	4 minutes	asks each candidate to talk about two visuals for 1 minute	**expresses opinions through comparing**	Organising an extended piece of discourse: • comparing • expressing opinions • speculating
3. Collaborative task	4 minutes	asks candidates to talk together using visual prompts	exchanges ideas and opinions, makes suggestions, agrees, disagrees, and **initiates discussion**	Sustaining an interaction: • exchanging ideas • inviting and responding to opinions • agreeing and/or disagreeing • suggesting • speculating • evaluating through negotiation, etc. • reaching a decision
4. Discussion on topics related to Part 3	4 minutes	**leads a discussion**	**exchanges views and opinions**	• expressing and justifying opinions • agreeing and/or disagreeing

■ Task Three: about the CAE Speaking test

Ask the students to read the statements and write 'True' or 'False' next to each one.

Answers

1. You can choose to take the test in a pair or a group of three. – **FALSE**. However, if there is an odd number of candidates at the centre, the last test of the session will be a group of three.

2. The assessor asks you questions during the test. – **FALSE**. The interlocutor asks the questions.

3. Only the assessor awards marks. – **FALSE**. The assessor gives detailed marks on grammar, vocabulary, discourse management, pronunciation and interactive communication but the interlocutor also gives a global mark.

4. You are given your marks at the end of the test. – **FALSE**. Examiners are not allowed to give any indication of a candidate's performance at the end of the test, and candidates should be discouraged from asking.

5. You might not know your partner. – **TRUE**. At open and devolved centres candidates may be paired at random.

6. You are not tested on your general knowledge. – **TRUE**. This is a test of language, not of general knowledge.

7. In Part 1, you ask your partner questions. – **FALSE**. You are asked direct questions by the interlocutor.

8. In Part 2, if your partner runs out of things to say you can help. – **FALSE**. Part 2 is the time when candidates can speak alone and uninterrupted. However, the listening candidate is asked a question at the end of their partner's long turn.

9. The questions are written at the top of the page in Parts 2 and 3. – **TRUE**. The questions are written at the top of the page with the visuals in the Candidate Booklet to help candidates remember and focus on the task.

10. You interact with your partner in both Parts 3 and 4. – **TRUE**. It is important in Part 3 that candidates interact with each other, and in Part 4 the interlocutor may address a question to both candidates for them to discuss. It is also possible in Part 4 for a candidate to add something to what their partner has said.

 Tell the students to check their answers with a partner. Then play the DVD and tell them to check if they were right.

CAE Speaking test
Teacher's Notes

This worksheet is based on Part 1 of the CAE Speaking test.

■ Task One

1. Tell the students to read the questions on the worksheet. Suggest that they work with a partner and ask and answer the questions in turn.
   - Where are you from?
   - How long have you been studying English?
   - What do you enjoy most about learning English?
   - What are your interests and leisure activities?
   - What's your happiest memory of school?
   - If you had an opportunity to learn something new, what would you choose?
   - Would you consider living abroad permanently?
   - Are you someone who likes to plan for the future or do you prefer to let things happen?
   - What part of the day do you enjoy most?
   - What do you like to do at weekends?

   Answers will depend on the students themselves and what they say.

 2. Play Part 1 on the DVD. Ask the students to discuss how their answers were different from Marie's and Chloe's.

   Answers will depend on the students themselves and what they say. Encourage students to think about how well they answered the questions, and how they feel about the way the candidates on the DVD answered the questions.

■ Task Two

 Play Part 1 on the DVD again. Ask the students to answer the questions on the worksheet.

Answers

1. How many questions are given to both candidates? Which ones? – The first and last. ('Where are you from?', 'What do you like to do at weekends?')
2. How does the interlocutor indicate who should answer a question? – She uses their names.
3. Which candidate speaks the most? – They are given an equal number of questions, but Marie extends her answers well.
4. How does Marie extend her answers? – By giving reasons. She often answers the question clearly, but then gives the reason with 'because' and provides more detail.
5. What does Marie say about sport and leisure? – She compares her feeling about it now with the past.
6. How could Chloe have improved her answers to the questions about learning and school? – She could have given reasons for what she wanted to study.
7. Who answers the last question about weekends best, Marie or Chloe? Why? – Chloe gives more detail, and Marie more or less repeats the same things. If Marie had added a different comment, it would have given her more opportunity to show the examiners what she can do.

■ Task Three

1. Tell the students to think of two questions to ask their partner in each of the topic areas.

- sports
- leisure interests
- work and study
- family
- travel and holidays
- entertainment
- experiences
- daily life
- future plans

2. Tell the students to practise in pairs or small groups, taking turns to ask and answer questions. Encourage them to extend their answers in an interesting way, and to use a range of grammar and interesting vocabulary. Remind them that this part requires personal answers, and personal information and ideas.

TEACHING TIPS FOR PART 1

1. In class give students regular opportunities to practise talking about themselves and what they think about different things. You can do this at the start or end of a lesson, by giving students a topic from the news to discuss briefly.

2. Have a box of cards with topics written on them, and do a quick 'warmer' activity regularly at the start of a lesson. Ask a student to pick out a topic card, divide students into small groups and give them 5 minutes to discuss the topic. Ask one student in the group to monitor the discussion and language used and suggest other ways of making suggestions or expressing opinions.

3. Ask students to prepare a short personal statement about their lives. (You could use questions from the *CAE Handbook for teachers* Part 1 to help them). Students could then exchange statements and ask each other more detailed questions about them.

4. Encourage students to use a variety of tenses whenever they have a discussion in class, and to use a range of vocabulary wherever possible. You could ask students to paraphrase what they have said, and use the Use of English key word transformations to encourage students to express themselves in a variety of ways.

HELPFUL HINTS FOR STUDENTS FOR PART 1

Apart from saying 'hello', **don't talk** to the assessor. The assessor will just listen to you and takes no part in the interaction.

Always try to answer the interlocutor's questions by giving some extra information, clarification or reasons.

Don't just give one-word answers. This does not give a very good impression and you want to show the assessor what you can do right from the start!

Always listen to your partner's answers because the interlocutor may ask you both the same question. It's a good idea to disagree and have something different to say or to agree and to add to what your partner has said.

Remember to speak clearly and loudly enough so that both examiners can hear you.

Take a deep breath and relax before you go into the exam room. This will help you to feel more confident.

CAE Speaking test
Teacher's Notes

WORKSHEET
2

This worksheet is based on Part 2 of the CAE Speaking test. Use the candidate visuals provided with this book or, before the lesson print out the Part 2 photographs (preferably in colour) from the DVD and make sure you have enough copies to give one set to each pair of students.

■ Task One: focus on Marie

1. Play the beginning of Part 2 on the DVD and stop it after the interlocutor has given Marie her task. Tell the students to listen carefully to the interlocutor's instructions to Marie and write the missing information in the box on the worksheet.

Answer

> *Interlocutor:* Marie, it's your turn first. Here are your pictures. They show **people travelling by train**.
>
> I'd like you to compare two of the pictures and say **what aspect of train travel they show**, and **how the people might be feeling**.

2. Ask the students what question they think the interlocutor will ask Chloe after Marie has spoken. Tell them to write it in the box on the worksheet.

3. Ask the students to work with a partner and take it in turns to do Marie's task. Tell them to discuss the questions on the worksheet.
   - Did you speak for a minute?
   - Did you compare two pictures in an organised way and answer the second part of the task?

4. Ask the students to watch Marie doing the task on the DVD but stop the recording after Marie's long turn and Chloe's response question. Ask the students to compare their performances with Marie's.

Answers

   - Does Marie answer the task, or just describe the pictures? – She just describes the pictures, and doesn't organise her answer very well.
   - How could she have done better? – She should have used the task to focus her answer more.

Ask the students if they were right about Chloe's question.

> *Interlocutor:* Chloe, which picture do you think **best shows the advantages of travelling by train?**

■ Task Two: focus on Chloe

1. Play the next part of Part 2 on the DVD. Tell the students to listen carefully to the interlocutor's instructions to Chloe and write the missing information in the box on the worksheet. Stop the DVD after the interlocutor has given Chloe her task.

Answer

> *Interlocutor:* Now, Chloe, here are your pictures. They show **people talking face to face**.
>
> I'd like you to compare two of the pictures and say **why these people might be talking to each other** and **how they might be feeling**.

2. Ask the students what question they think the interlocutor will ask Marie after Chloe has spoken. Tell them to write it in the box on the worksheet.

3. Ask the students to work with a partner and take it in turns to do Chloe's task. Tell them to discuss the questions on the worksheet.
   - Did you speak for a minute?
   - Did you compare two pictures in an organised way, and answer the second part of the task?

4. Ask the students to watch Chloe doing the task on the DVD. Ask them to compare their performances with hers.

   Answers
   - Does Chloe address the task? – Yes.
   - Does Chloe use a range of structures, particularly tenses? – No – she tends to use the present tenses all the time.

   Ask the students if they were right about Marie's question.

Interlocutor:	Marie, **which of these people do you think know each other the best?**

■ Task Three

1. Play the whole of Part 2 again, and tell the students to complete the table on the worksheet.

   Answers

Question	Marie	Chloe
What does she do first?	She describes the pictures.	Identifies the pictures she wants to talk about, then compares them.
What does she do next?	She continues to describe the pictures.	She addresses the task.
Does she use a range of tenses?	No – it's mostly the present tense.	No, she uses the present tense.
Does she use a range of vocabulary?	Not really, because she is just describing the pictures and not addressing the speculative element of the task.	It is adequate for the task.
Does she address the task?	No.	Yes.
Does she give an appropriate response to her listening candidate question?	Yes – she gives her opinion and then supports it with reasons.	Yes – it is a good length and quite well organised.

2. Ask the students to discuss the question on the worksheet.
   - Who gives a better performance in this task, Marie or Chloe. Why?

   Answer

   Chloe, because she is more organised in her answer, and addresses the task. Marie just describes the pictures and doesn't address the task. However, neither of them really demonstrates a good range of structures.

■ Useful phrases

Below are some useful phrases which may be helpful for students when comparing the photos, but students should take care not to overuse them.

Comparing	Both of these . . . Neither of these . . . One of these . . ., while the other . . . This one . . ., but on the other hand that one . . . This picture . . . whereas the other . . .
Speculating	It seems to me that . . . It's hard to say, but I think . . . It looks like a . . . I'd say . . . It must/might/could/can't be . . . It must/might/could have been . . . I don't think it . . ., because . . .
Expressing opinions	Personally speaking, . . . Speaking personally, . . . Personally, I . . . I've never thought about it, but I suppose . . . I don't really like . . ., but if I had to choose . . . It's very difficult to say, but I think . . . It seems to me that . . .

TEACHING TIPS FOR PART 2

1. Set aside time in class to practise Part 2 so that your students can get used to speculating about visuals and can give each other help and support while they practise.

2. In class, students could practise the activity in pairs, timing each other to see how it feels to talk for a minute on their own. Remind them to speculate about the pictures using the prompts written on the paper, and not just to describe them.

3. Point out to students how important it is:
   - to organise their thoughts clearly so that they make the most of their time
   - to try and complete the task the examiner asks them to do (which is written on the paper with the visuals)
   - not to worry about the timing in the examination but just to keep talking until the examiner says 'Thank you'.

4. You could also do activities in which:
   - students bring in their own pictures and try to link them thematically by making suggestions and speculating about possible connections
   - students are given a topic which they have to talk about for a minute.

5. Give students strategies for starting and ending their talk.

HELPFUL HINTS FOR STUDENTS FOR PART 2

Ask the interlocutor for clarification if you are unsure about what to do.

Begin speaking immediately; don't waste time thinking about what you are going to say.

Concentrate on the task; don't just describe the pictures. Remember that the task is written on the paper for you to refer to.

Don't panic if you don't know the word for something – paraphrase it and move on.

Don't interrupt while your partner is talking.

Even if you have no opinion about the task, invent one.

Try to keep talking for as long as you can. Don't stop before your minute is over!

Remember not to worry if the interlocutor stops you. To make the test fair, each candidate is given the same amount of talking time.

This worksheet is based on Part 3 of the CAE Speaking test. Use the candidate visuals provided with this book or, before the lesson, print out the Part 3 pictures (preferably in colour) from the DVD and make sure you have enough copies to give one set to each pair of students.

■ Task One

1. Play the beginning of Part 3 on the DVD. Tell the students to listen carefully to the interlocutor's instructions and write the missing information in the box on the worksheet.

Answers

> *Interlocutor:* Now I'd like you to talk about something together for about 3 minutes.
>
> Here are some pictures showing **different ways in which computers affect our lives**.
>
> First, talk to each other about **how these pictures show the role of computers nowadays**.
>
> Then decide **which picture best reflects the difference computers have made to our lives**.

2. Tell the students to work with a partner and do the task. Remind them to spend 3 minutes discussing all the pictures.

3. Ask the students to discuss the questions on the worksheet with a partner. When they have finished, answer any general questions they have about the task.
   • Did you have time to discuss all the pictures?
   • Did you have something to say about all the pictures?
   • Did you find any pictures easy or difficult to talk about?
   • Did you reach a decision too early and leave yourselves with nothing else to talk about?

4. Now play all of Part 3 on the DVD. Ask the students to compare their performances with Marie's and Chloe's.

■ Task Two

Play Part 3 on the DVD again. Ask the students to answer the questions on the worksheet.

Answers

1. Who starts the discussion? How does she do this? – Marie. She talks about the first picture.
2. Who responds the most? – Equal. They don't ask each other questions but they pick up on what the other one has said, and both initiate discussion.
3. How do Marie and Chloe interact with each other? – They make suggestions or statements and then add detail. They could ask one another more what they think.
4. Do they seem interested in what their partner is saying? – Yes. They pick up on what each other says, but they could look at each other more.
5. Do they look at the interlocutor? Is this a good thing? – Yes, they do look at the interlocutor, but this is not a good thing as they should be talking to each other. It is better if candidates talk to each other and ignore the interlocutor in this part of the test.
6. Does the interlocutor ask them questions during the task? – No.
7. Who speaks the most during Part 3? – They speak equally, but they don't actually interact with each other very much.
8. Do they take turns, or does one person dominate the discussion? – They take turns to initiate discussion, but they don't actually ask one another questions or invite one another to speak.
9. Do they speak about all the pictures? – Yes.
10. Do they reach a decision? Does this matter? – Yes, they do but it doesn't matter if candidates don't do this. The discussion is more important than the decision.

■ Task Three

1. Play Part 3 on the DVD again. Ask the students to complete the table on the worksheet. Tell them to note down some examples of the language Marie and Chloe use.

Answers

Language to:	Marie	Chloe
agree/disagree	Yes, it's not just for companies . . .	Yes, it shows that . . .
move the task forward	These three pictures are . . . and these three pictures are . . .	Let me see . . . And what makes the difference in our lives?

2. Ask the students to discuss the questions on the worksheet with a partner.

Answers

- How much do Marie and Chloe interact with each other? – Not enough – they just say what they want to say, and don't invite one another to speak. They are obviously listening to one another, though, because they pick up on what their partner says.
- What do you think they could do to interact with each other more? – Ask one another what they think.

■ Useful phrases

Below are some useful phrases which may be helpful for students when doing this task, but students should take care not to overuse them.

Initiating/focusing on the task	So we have to . . . There are several possibilities for . . . Let's talk about . . . first, shall we? Let's see what the good points are, shall we? I think they/we will/would need to . . . We have to choose . . . We have to decide which . . .
Expressing opinions/ views/ideas	What do you think about . . . ? It seems to me that . . . I think . . . What do you think? From what I know . . . In my opinion . . . As far as I'm concerned . . . Personally speaking . . . Could I just add that . . . ? If I might come in here . . . Don't you think . . . ? I've heard . . . I'm sure . . .
Agreeing/disagreeing	That's a good point. I couldn't have put it better myself. I couldn't agree more. I'm sure you're right. I hadn't thought of that. What a good idea! Exactly! I see what you mean, but don't you think . . . ? Yes, but isn't it true that . . . ? I'm sure that's wrong. I don't think I would go along with that . . . You have a point there, but I think . . . I think that might be a bit difficult if . . . I'm sorry but I can't agree. That's a good point but . . .
Concluding	So, if we summarise . . . So, what shall we decide? So, what do you think? I think we agree. So, what shall we say? Right, so you think . . . and I think . . . Can we agree . . .? Don't we agree . . .? So, shall we agree to disagree? Is that how you see it? So if I've understood correctly, we've decided on . . . so far.

1. As well as general vocabulary, the students will need to be taught the language for:
   - turn-taking
   - negotiating
   - making suggestions and initiating discussion
   - exchanging ideas and opinions
   - justifying opinions and giving reasons for ideas
   - ranking and prioritising
   - evaluating
   - selecting

2. Students should take part in regular discussions in class, either in pairs, small groups or as a whole class. They should focus on the phrases they use for the functions identified in 1).

3. Use radio and TV discussion programmes and podcasts of radio phone-ins as examples of the functions identified in 1).

4. *Class suggestions*
   Choose a topic or write a statement on the board. Ask students to list five advantages and five disadvantages or five points for and five against the statement. Then get them to discuss these in groups and try to rank them in importance.

5. *Individual suggestions*
   Encourage students to improve their knowledge of general issues by reading English-language newspapers and magazines, watching English language programmes on TV, listening to the radio or downloading podcasts of any topic that interests them. This will give them ideas for things to say, and help them to form their own opinions about things.

Remind students that:
- there is no right or wrong answer to this task
- examiners are listening to the quality of language used and it is not necessary for students to actually reach a decision
- students must have something to say – although candidates are not being assessed on their knowledge of the world, if they don't actually express any ideas or opinions, it will be difficult for the examiners to give a fair appraisal of their language ability.

Ask for clarification if you are unsure about what to do, but remember that your partner can also help you with the task.

Begin immediately; don't waste time thinking about what you are going to say.

Remember that the task is written on the paper for you to refer to.

Don't panic if you don't know the word for something – paraphrase it, or ask your partner if they know the word.

Say as much as you can about each visual in relation to the task before you move on to the next one. Try to use a variety of language if you can.

If you have no opinion about one of the visuals, ask your partner or speculate about the picture in relation to the task.

Remember to work together with your partner. You use different types of language when you speak by yourself and when you speak with another person, so working together with your partner will allow you to use a greater range of language.

Try to take it in turns to initiate discussion – don't just respond to what your partner says.

You are not being assessed on what you say, but the way you say it. This is a language exam, not a test of general knowledge.

This worksheet is based on Part 4 of the CAE Speaking test.

■ Task One

1. Direct the students to the five questions on the worksheet. Ask them to work with a partner and discuss each question in turn.
   - Some people say that computers are helping to create a generation without social skills. What's your opinion?
   - What are the advantages and disadvantages of shopping by computer?
   - How far do you agree that the computer is the greatest invention of modern times?
   - A lot of personal information about all of us is now kept on computers. Do you find this worrying?
   - In future, what role do you think there will be for people who are not interested in technology?

   This will depend on how students deal with the questions. Encourage them to extend their answers as much as possible.

 2. Play Part 4 on the DVD and ask students to compare their answers with Marie's and Chloe's.

■ Task Two

 Play Part 4 again and ask the students to answer the questions on the worksheet. Invite general comments about Marie's and Chloe's performance.

Answers

1. Does the interlocutor ask each candidate the same questions? – Not exactly. She doesn't repeat the question but asks the second candidate e.g. 'Do you agree?' and 'How about you?'.
2. Does the interlocutor ask candidates to answer questions individually, or discuss them together? – Both. She addresses the first two questions to the candidates individually, but asks the other candidate to add something. She addresses Question 3 to both candidates.
3. Do the candidates only speak when asked by the interlocutor? – No. They contribute ideas when they want to, and agree and disagree with each other.
4. How does the interlocutor encourage discussion between the candidates? – By using hand gestures.
5. How do candidates extend their answers? – By giving reasons and details about their ideas.
6. How does the interlocutor finish the test? – 'Thank you. That's the end of the test.'

■ Task Three

1. What is the difference between the direct questions candidates are asked in Part 1 and those in Part 4? Ask the students to complete the sentences on their worksheet with the information from the box.

personal information	both candidates	an individual candidate	opinions

Answers

a) Part 1 questions ask for **personal information** but Part 4 questions ask for **opinions**.
b) Part 1 questions are addressed to **an individual candidate** but Part 4 questions can be addressed to **both candidates**.

2. Ask the students to decide, using the information above, which of the questions in the box are from Part 1 and which are from Part 4.

Answers

Questions	Which part?
Some people say the problem with the world today is that people only care about themselves. What's your opinion?	Part 4
What do you enjoy learning?	Part 1
Do you think it's better to give money to local organisations or national organisations? Why?	Part 4
What might you be doing this time next year?	Part 1
What kinds of problems can having a lot of money sometimes cause?	Part 4
What kinds of holiday appeal to you most?	Part 1
Do you think you would like to work in the travel industry?	Part 1
How important do you think money is for a happy life?	Part 4
What's the most exciting experience you've ever had?	Part 1
What can we all do as individuals to protect the environment?	Part 4

3. Tell students to think about the kind of language they need to use for questions in each part. They have to decide which phrases in the box below would be most useful for Part 1, and which for Part 4.

Answers

Language for Part 1	Language for Part 4
I'd like . . . That's definitely something I'd like to do . . . It has to be . . . That's something I've always wanted to do.	In my opinion . . . What I think about that is . . . I'd never thought about that before, but . . . I'd have to agree with that idea . . .

■ Useful phrases

Below are some useful phrases which may be helpful for students when doing this part of the test, but students should take care not to overuse them.

Offering a tentative opinion	I'm not sure . . . Probably . . . Perhaps . . . Maybe . . . It's very difficult . . ., but I think . . . It's not something I feel very strongly about, but . . .
Developing the discussion	I'd like to add something . . . There's something else I'd like to say . . . I couldn't have put it better myself.
Offering a strong opinion	Actually, I feel quite strongly that . . . I'm quite certain that . . . I know for a fact that . . . I really don't think it is right that . . .
Expressing agreement	Could I just add that . . . ? Exactly!

1. Part 4 is a continuation of Part 3, and candidates will be asked questions to extend the discussion of the topic they discussed in Part 3. Candidates should be prepared to:
   - give their opinion on questions put by the interlocutor
   - extend their responses by giving reasons and further details
   - agree or disagree with their partner, giving reasons and justifying their ideas
   - add to or extend their partner's response appropriately
   - ask a question to confirm or seek information
   - interact with their partner and not dominate the conversation.

2. Parts 3 and 4 both involve discussion. It is important that teachers give their students as much practice in taking part in a discussion as possible. They should tell their students not to be afraid of giving opinions, interrupting or disagreeing, but remind them that they should do this sensitively and politely.

3. Encourage students to develop their own opinions by bringing in articles of interest from the news and getting other students to ask them questions about it.

4. As many topics as possible should be covered in class. The following topics are examples:
   - education and studies
   - holidays and leisure
   - past and present
   - transport and travel
   - jobs and work
   - issues around the environment
   - climate and weather

Listen to what your partner says, and offer additional ideas or information where appropriate.

Remember that you don't always have to agree with your partner – it makes an interesting discussion if you have a different opinion.

Be aware that the interlocutor may address some questions to you individually, but may also ask you to discuss a question with your partner. In this case, turn to your partner and be prepared to express your own opinion and ask them what they think.

CAE Speaking test
Teacher's Notes

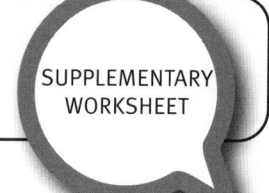

SUPPLEMENTARY WORKSHEET

■ How we assess speaking for CAE

Candidates are assessed on their own individual performance and not in relation to each other, according to the following five analytical criteria: grammatical resource, vocabulary resource, discourse management, pronunciation and interactive communication. These criteria are interpreted at CAE level. Assessment is based on performance in the whole test, and is not related to performance in particular parts of the test.

Both examiners assess the candidates. The assessor applies detailed analytical scales, and the interlocutor applies a global achievement scale, which is based on the analytical scale.

■ Analytical scales

Grammatical resource

This refers to the accurate and appropriate use of a range of both simple and complex forms. Performance is viewed in terms of the overall effectiveness of the language used in spoken interaction.

Vocabulary resource

This refers to the candidate's ability to use a range of vocabulary to meet task requirements. At CAE level, the tasks require candidates to speculate and exchange views on unfamiliar topics. Performance is viewed in terms of the overall effectiveness of the language used in spoken interaction.

Discourse management

This refers to the candidate's ability to link utterances together to form coherent speech, without undue hesitation. The utterances should be relevant to the tasks, and should be arranged logically to develop the themes or arguments required by the tasks.

Pronunciation

This refers to the candidate's ability to produce comprehensible utterances to fulfil the task requirements. This includes stress and intonation as well as individual sounds. Examiners put themselves in the position of a non-ESOL specialist and assess the overall impact of the pronunciation and the degree of effort required to understand the candidate.

Interactive communication

This refers to the candidate's ability to take an active part in the development of the discourse. This requires an ability to participate in the range of interactive situations in the test and to develop discussions on a range of topics by initiating and responding appropriately. This also refers to the deployment of strategies to maintain interaction at an appropriate level throughout the test so that the tasks can be fulfilled.

■ Global achievement scale

This refers to the candidate's overall performance in dealing with the tasks in the four separate parts of the CAE Speaking test. The global mark is an independent impression mark which reflects the assessment of the candidate's performance from the interlocutor's perspective.

■ CAE typical minimum adequate performance

The candidate develops the interaction with contributions which are mostly coherent and extended when dealing with the CAE-level tasks. Grammar is mostly accurate and vocabulary appropriate. Utterances are understood with very little strain on the listener.

Please note:
Candidates cannot pass or fail any individual paper. The candidate's grade for the examination is based on their total score from all five papers.

■ Assessment task

Answers

Grammatical resource	Use a range of structures. Try not to make basic mistakes.
Vocabulary resource	Try to use interesting words, not just the same ones all the time. Try to be precise in the words you use.
Discourse management	Try to connect your ideas together clearly. Try to develop your ideas logically and fluently.
Pronunciation	Don't worry too much if you have an accent, but try to use correct word stress and intonation. Think about your listener – how can you help them to understand what you are saying?
Interactive communication	Participate in all parts of the test actively. Remember to ask questions as well as respond.

NOTES

CAE Speaking test
Student Worksheets

This section contains the six Student Worksheets for CAE:
- Introductory Worksheet – provides an introduction to the CAE Speaking test as a whole
- Worksheet 1 – based on Part 1 of the CAE Speaking test
- Worksheet 2 – based on Part 2 of the CAE Speaking test
- Worksheet 3 – based on Part 3 of the CAE Speaking test
- Worksheet 4 – based on Part 4 of the CAE Speaking test
- Supplementary Worksheet – explains how the CAE Speaking test is assessed.

The Student Worksheet pages of this book are photocopiable and you can also print copies from the Student Worksheets folder on the DVD. For your class you will also need:
- the DVD
- for Parts 2 and 3, the candidate visuals. You can find one set of these inside the front and back covers of this book. There is also a folder on the DVD with the candidate visuals if you want to print more copies and have access to a colour printer.

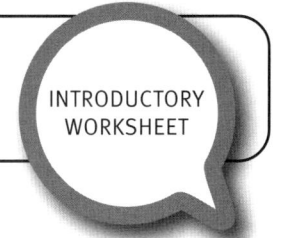
■ Aims of the DVD and worksheets

- to raise your awareness of the format of the CAE Speaking test
- to focus your attention on techniques that will improve your performance
- to provide opportunities for you to practise the language used in the different parts of the test.

Please note:

The DVD and worksheets are not intended as a forum for discussing grades. Although in certain questions we are asking you to look at the candidates' performance, it is with a view to improving your own performance and not for you to grade the candidates on the DVD.

The CAE Speaking test on the DVD has been produced for teaching purposes only and is not a live exam. There are therefore, no grades available.

Some of the answers to the activities in the worksheets cannot be found on the DVD.

Student's Introductory Worksheet

Before watching the DVD, test your knowledge of the CAE Speaking test by completing as much of the following worksheet as you can. Check your answers with a partner and then watch the DVD. You can find some of the information you need on the Candidate Support site at **www.candidates.CambridgeESOL.org/cs/Help_with_exams/General_English/CAE** and in the *Information for Candidates* booklet which you can download.

■ Task One: general information about the CAE Speaking test

Fill in the missing information:

1. Length: _____ minutes

2. Normal format: _____ candidates and _____ examiners

3. Number of parts: _____

4. The Speaking test is worth _____% of the whole CAE exam (all papers).

■ Task Two: what happens in the CAE Speaking test

Complete the table with the missing information from the box below.

• leads a discussion • exchanges views and opinions • asks individual direct questions	• expresses opinions through comparing • gives personal information • initiates discussion

Parts	Timing	What the interlocutor does	What a candidate does
1. Interview	3 minutes	_____ _____	_____ _____
2. Individual long turn	4 minutes	asks each candidate to talk about two visuals for 1 minute	_____ _____
3. Collaborative task	4 minutes	asks candidates to talk together using visual prompts	exchanges ideas and opinions, makes suggestions, agrees, disagrees, and _____ _____
4. Discussion on topics related to Part 3	4 minutes	_____ _____	_____ _____

■ Task Three: about the CAE Speaking test

Read the following statements and write 'True' or 'False' next to each one:

1. You can choose to take the test in a pair or a group of three. _____

2. The assessor asks you questions during the test. _____

3. Only the assessor awards marks. _____

4. You are given your marks at the end of the test. _____

5. You might not know your partner. _____

6. You are not tested on your general knowledge. _____

7. In Part 1, you ask your partner questions. _____

8. In Part 2, if your partner runs out of things to say you can help. _____

9. The questions are written at the top of the page in Parts 2 and 3. _____

10. You interact with your partner in both Parts 3 and 4. _____

 Check your answers with a partner. Then watch the whole Speaking test on the DVD to see if you were right.

This worksheet is based on Part 1 of the CAE Speaking test.

■ Task One

1. Read the questions below. Work with a partner and ask and answer them in turn.
   - Where are you from?
   - How long have you been studying English?
   - What do you enjoy most about learning English?
   - What are your interests and leisure activities?
   - What's your happiest memory of school?
   - If you had an opportunity to learn something new, what would you choose?
   - Would you consider living abroad permanently?
   - Are you someone who likes to plan for the future or do you prefer to let things happen?
   - What part of the day do you enjoy most?
   - What do you like to do at weekends?

 2. Now watch Marie and Chloe do Part 1 on the DVD. How were your answers different from theirs?

■ Task Two

 Watch Part 1 on the DVD again and answer the following questions:

1. How many questions are given to both candidates? Which ones?

   _____

   _____

2. How does the interlocutor indicate who should answer a question?

   _____

   _____

3. Which candidate speaks the most?

   _____

   _____

4. How does Marie extend her answers?

   _____

   _____

5. What does Marie say about sport and leisure?

   _____

   _____

6. How could Chloe have improved her answers to the questions about learning and school?

   _____

   _____

7. Who answers the last question about weekends best, Marie or Chloe? Why?

   _____

   _____

■ Task Three

1. Look at the topic areas below. Think of two questions to ask your partner in each area.

- sports
- leisure interests
- work and study
- family
- travel and holidays
- entertainment
- experiences
- daily life
- future plans

You can write your questions in the box below if you like.

Topic area	My questions
_____	1. _____ 2. _____
_____	1. _____ 2. _____
_____	1. _____ 2. _____
_____	1. _____ 2. _____
_____	1. _____ 2. _____
_____	1. _____ 2. _____
_____	1. _____ 2. _____

2. Now practise in pairs or small groups, taking turns to ask your partner(s) your questions, and answer their questions.

 **UNIVERSITY** *of* **CAMBRIDGE**
ESOL Examinations

CAE Speaking test
Student Worksheets

 WORKSHEET **2**

This worksheet is based on Part 2 of the CAE Speaking test.

■ Task One: focus on Marie

 1. Watch the beginning of Part 2 on the DVD and listen carefully to the interlocutor's instructions to Marie. Write the missing information in the box below.

> *Interlocutor:* Marie, it's your turn first. Here are your pictures. They show _____
>
> _____ .
>
> I'd like you to compare two of the pictures and say _____
>
> and _____ .

2. What question do you think the interlocutor will ask Chloe? Write your idea in the box below.

> *Interlocutor:* Chloe, which picture do you think _____ ?

3. Now work with a partner and take it in turns to do Marie's task. Then discuss these questions with your partner:
   - Did you speak for a minute?
   - Did you compare two pictures in an organised way and answer the second part of the task?

 4. Now watch Marie do the task on the DVD and compare your performance with hers. These questions will help you:
   - Does Marie do the task, or just describe the pictures?
   - How could she have done better?
   - How does your question for Chloe (above) compare with the question the interlocutor asks Chloe?

■ Task Two: focus on Chloe

 1. Watch the next part of Part 2 and listen carefully to the interlocutor's instructions to Chloe. Write the missing information in the box below.

> *Interlocutor:* Now, Chloe, here are your pictures. They show _____
>
> _____ .
>
> I'd like you to compare two of the pictures and say _____
>
> and _____ .

2. What question do you think the interlocutor will ask Marie? Write your idea in the box below.

> *Interlocutor:* Marie, _____ ?

3. Now work with a partner and take it in turns to do Chloe's task. Then discuss these questions:
   - Did you speak for a minute?
   - Did you compare two pictures in an organised way, and answer the second part of the task?

4. Now watch Chloe do the task on the DVD and compare your performance with hers. Discuss these questions with your partner:
   - Does Chloe address the task?
   - Does Chloe use a range of structures, particularly tenses?
   - How does your question for Marie (on the previous page) compare with the question the interlocutor asks Marie?

■ Task Three

1. Watch the whole of Part 2 again, and complete the table below.

Question	Marie	Chloe
What does she do first?		
What does she do next?		
Does she use a range of tenses?		
Does she use a range of vocabulary?		
Does she address the task?		
Does she give an appropriate response to her listening candidate question?		

2. Who gives a better performance in this task, Marie or Chloe? Why?

_____

_____

UNIVERSITY *of* CAMBRIDGE
ESOL Examinations

CAE Speaking test
Student Worksheets

WORKSHEET

3

This worksheet is based on Part 3 of the CAE Speaking test.

■ Task One

1. Watch the beginning of Part 3 on the DVD and listen carefully to the interlocutor's instructions. Write the missing information in the box below.

Interlocutor:	Now I'd like you to talk about something together for about 3 minutes.
	Here are some pictures showing _____ .
	First, talk to each other about _____
	_____ .
	Then decide _____ .

2. Work with a partner and do the task above. Make sure that you spend 3 minutes discussing all the pictures.

3. Discuss these questions with your partner:
   - Did you have time to discuss all the pictures?
   - Did you have something to say about all the pictures?
   - Did you find any pictures easy or difficult to talk about?
   - Did you reach a decision too early and leave yourselves with nothing else to talk about?

4. Now watch Marie and Chloe do the task on the DVD and compare your performance with theirs.

■ Task Two

Watch Marie and Chloe on the DVD again and answer the following questions:

1. Who starts the discussion? How does she do this?

   _____

2. Who responds the most?

   _____

3. How do Marie and Chloe interact with each other?

   _____

4. Do they seem interested in what their partner is saying?

   _____

5. Do they look at the interlocutor? Is this a good thing?

   _____

6. Does the interlocutor ask them questions during the task?

   _____

7. Who speaks the most during Part 3?

   _____

8. Do they take turns, or does one person dominate the discussion?

_____

9. Do they speak about all the pictures?

_____

10. Do they reach a decision? Does this matter?

_____

■ Task Three

1. Now watch Part 3 of the test again, and complete the table below.

   Note down some examples of the language Marie and Chloe use.

Language to:	Marie uses:	Chloe uses:
agree/disagree		
move the task forward		

2. Discuss these questions with a partner:
   - How much do Marie and Chloe interact with each other?
   - What do you think they could do to interact with each other more?

This worksheet is based on Part 4 of the CAE Speaking test.

■ Task One

1. Here are five questions related to the topic of computers which you discussed in Part 3. Work with a partner and discuss each one in turn.
   - Some people say that computers are helping to create a generation without social skills. What's your opinion?
   - What are the advantages and disadvantages of shopping by computer?
   - How far do you agree that the computer is the greatest invention of modern times?
   - A lot of personal information about all of us is now kept on computers. Do you find this worrying?
   - In future, what role do you think there will be for people who are not interested in technology?

2. Now watch Marie and Chloe do Part 4 on the DVD and compare your answers with theirs.

■ Task Two

Watch Part 4 again and answer the following questions:

1. Does the interlocutor ask each candidate the same questions?

   _____

2. Does the interlocutor ask candidates to answer questions individually, or discuss them together?

   _____

3. Do the candidates only speak when asked by the interlocutor?

   _____

4. How does the interlocutor encourage discussion between the candidates?

   _____

5. How do candidates extend their answers?

   _____

6. How does the interlocutor finish the test?

   _____

■ Task Three

1. What is the difference between the direct questions in Part 1 and the direct questions in Part 4? Complete the two sentences below with the information from the box.

personal information	both candidates	an individual candidate	opinions

   a) Part 1 questions ask for _____ but Part 4 questions ask for _____ .

   b) Part 1 questions are addressed to _____ but Part 4 questions can be addressed to _____ .

2. Using the information on the previous page, decide which of the questions in the box below are from Part 1 and which are from Part 4. Write your answers in the boxes on the right.

Questions	Which part?
Some people say the problem with the world today is that people only care about themselves. What's your opinion?	
What do you enjoy learning?	
Do you think it's better to give money to local organisations or national organisations? Why?	
What might you be doing this time next year?	
What kinds of problems can having a lot of money sometimes cause?	
What kinds of holiday appeal to you most?	
Do you think you would like to work in the travel industry?	
How important do you think money is for a happy life?	
What's the most exciting experience you've ever had?	
What can we all do as individuals to protect the environment?	

3. Think about the kind of language you need to use for questions in each part. Decide which phrases in the box below would be most useful for Part 1, and which for Part 4. Write your answers in the boxes on the right.

Phrase	Which part?
In my opinion . . .	
I'd like . . .	
What I think about that is . . .	
That's definitely something I'd like to do . . .	
I'd never thought about that before, but . . .	
It has to be . . .	
I'd have to agree with that idea.	
That's something I've always wanted to do.	

 **UNIVERSITY** *of* **CAMBRIDGE**
ESOL Examinations

CAE Speaking test
Student Worksheets

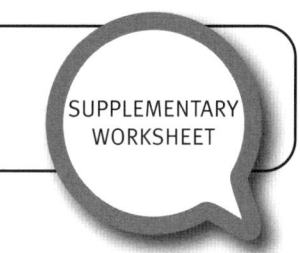 SUPPLEMENTARY
WORKSHEET

This worksheet helps you understand how we assess your speaking for CAE.

■ Assessment task

Here are 10 pieces of advice for getting good marks in each section of the assessment criteria, but they are jumbled up. Put them into the correct box.

- Use a range of structures.
- Remember to ask questions as well as respond.
- Try to develop your ideas logically and fluently.
- Try to use interesting words, not just the same ones all the time.
- Try to connect your ideas together clearly.
- Try to be precise in the words you use.
- Try not to make basic mistakes.
- Participate in all parts of the test actively.
- Don't worry too much if you have an accent, but try to use correct word stress and intonation.
- Think about your listener – how can you help them to understand what you are saying?

Grammatical resource	
Vocabulary resource	
Discourse management	
Pronunciation	
Interactive communication	

Dos and Don'ts checklist

■ **Throughout the test**

Do listen carefully to instructions given and questions asked throughout the test and focus your answers appropriately.

Do ask for clarification from the interlocutor only if you are not sure what you have been asked.

Do speak clearly so that both examiners can hear you.

Do make use of opportunities to speak in all parts of the test, and extend your answers where appropriate.

Don't worry about being interrupted by the interlocutor. It's important that the interlocutor keeps to the correct timing throughout the test.

■ **Part 1**

Do extend your answers appropriately by giving reasons or examples.

Do remember that these questions are about you and your personal opinions.

Don't prepare long responses in advance. You are unlikely to answer questions correctly.

Don't just answer 'yes' or 'no' as you will not demonstrate a range of language.

■ **Part 2**

Do use the written prompts on the paper to help you remember the task.

Do answer the question you are asked after your partner has spoken, but don't speak for too long – you have up to 30 seconds for your answer.

Don't interrupt your partner's long turn.

Don't worry about being interrupted by the interlocutor after you have spoken for a minute.

Don't try to give your views during your partner's long turn.

Don't just describe the photographs. Follow the interlocutor's instructions and answer the questions as this will help you produce language at the right level.

■ **Part 3**

Do use the written prompts on the paper to help you remember the task.

Do talk about each picture together in detail before moving on to the next.

Do respond to what your partner says before making new suggestions.

Do be sensitive to turn-taking.

Don't try to dominate your partner or interrupt them in an abrupt way.

Don't simply respond to what your partner says all the time. Be prepared to initiate discussion by asking questions and developing topics.

Don't worry if you disagree with your partner. As long as you are polite and not overbearing, this is all part of interactive communication.

Don't make your decision too early – it should come at the very end of your discussion.

■ **Part 4**

Do try to give extended answers wherever possible – give reasons and examples for what you think.

Do discuss answers with your partner when invited to do so by the interlocutor.

Do remember that you should give your opinions but there is no 'right' answer to the questions – you are assessed on your language not your ideas.

Don't worry if you disagree with your partner's ideas – you can show good language by disagreeing and giving reasons.

- How do these pictures show the role of computers nowadays?
- Which picture best reflects the difference computers have made to our lives?